D1000281

Alphabet Fun

# H Is for Honk!
## A Transportation Alphabet

by Catherine Ipcizade

CAPSTONE PRESS
a capstone imprint

# A is for
# ambulance.

An ambulance is a rescue vehicle. It takes sick or hurt people to the hospital quickly. Paramedics help sick people during the ride.

# B is for bicycle.

Some bicycles are made to race! Others are made for cruising. Either way, helmets keep riders safe.

3

# C is for car.

Cars take kids to school, adults to work, and families on vacations. Buckle up, everyone. Road trips are fun!

# D is for **driver**.

The driver guides a vehicle with the steering wheel. Her feet push the gas and brake pedals. Watch out! Drivers must be on the lookout for other cars.

# E is for electric car.

Electric cars don't need gasoline. They run on batteries. Electric cars plug into outlets. The electricity charges the batteries.

# F is for **fire truck**.

Sirens blast. Lights flash. A red fire truck races out of the fire station and down the street. Firefighters climb the tall ladder to rescue people from a burning building.

**G** is for **gas station**.

Fill 'er up! Cars and trucks get fuel at gas stations. A hose stretches from the gas pump to the car's gas tank. Gasoline goes through the hose and into the tank.

# H is for honk.

Honk! People honk their horns to avoid accidents. Honking tells other drivers to look out or move over.

# I is for interstate.

Interstates are long roads. They let people travel from state to state. Cars can go as fast as 80 miles (129 kilometers) per hour on some interstates.

# J is for junkyard.

Wrecked and old vehicles go to the junkyard. But some of their parts still work. People can buy these parts at the junkyard.

# K is for kayak.

A kayak is a long, thin boat. Kayakers sit with their legs stretched out in front of them. They use paddles to steer the boat down the river.

# L is for limousine.

Who's in that limousine? No one knows! Limos have dark windows and room for many people to sit. People rent limos for special events like weddings.

# M is for motorcycle.

Vroom! Riding a motorcycle takes balance like riding a bicycle. German engineer Gottlieb Daimler made the first gas-powered motorcycle in 1885.

**N** is for
**New York
subway system**.

Each weekday more than 5 million New Yorkers ride the subway. These underground trains run all through the city.

# O is for oil.

Engines need oil to run smoothly and stay clean. But changing the oil can be a messy job! First, the dirty oil is drained. The new oil is then carefully poured in.

# P is for police car.

A police car flashes its blue and red lights. Other drivers pull over to let the police car pass safely.

**Q** is for **quit**.

Sputter! Clank! Sometimes vehicles quit working. Mechanics use special tools to fix cars and trucks.

# R is for rocket.

3, 2, 1. Blast off! A rocket shoots a spaceship into the air. The crew on board are called astronauts. They work in space.

# S is for **school bus**.

All aboard! The yellow school bus takes students to and from school. Drivers can't miss the bright color of the bus. The color helps keep children safe.

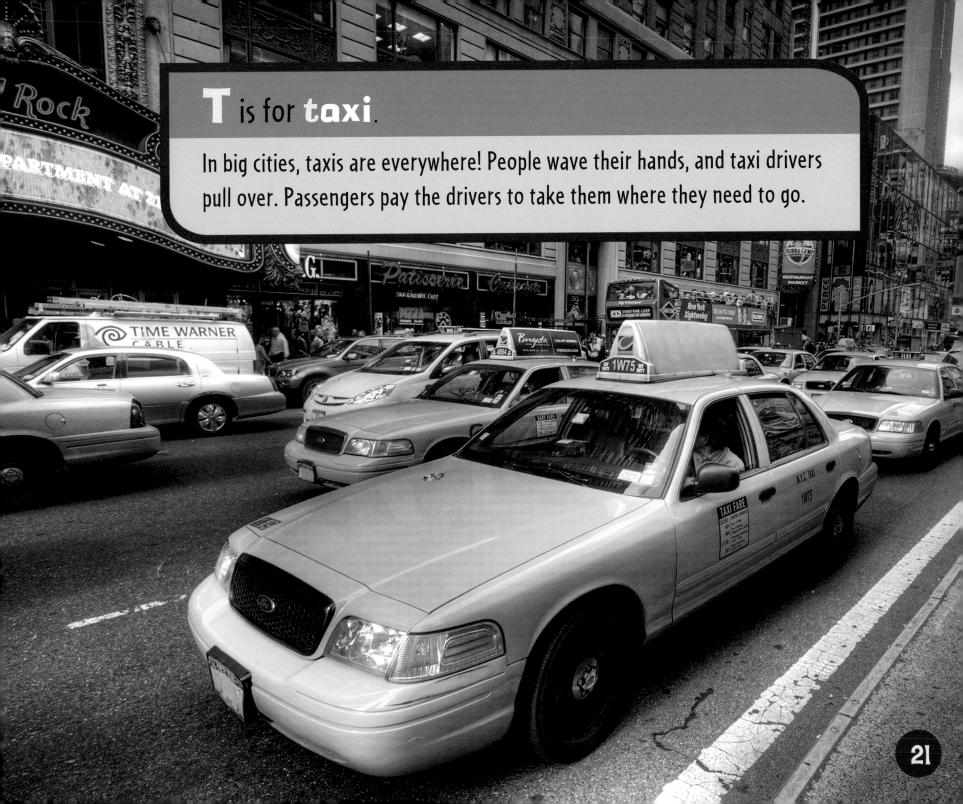

# T is for **taxi**.

In big cities, taxis are everywhere! People wave their hands, and taxi drivers pull over. Passengers pay the drivers to take them where they need to go.

# U is for up.

Hot air balloons take riders up, up, UP into the air. Passengers stand in the balloon basket. Flames shoot out of a burner above their heads. The heat makes the balloon rise.

**V** is for **van**.

Most cars can hold five people. But a van has room for eight. Minivans have three rows of seats for big families or lots of friends.

# W is for wing.

Airplanes need wings to fly. The wings are flat on the bottom and curved on the top. This shape helps airplanes lift off the ground and stay in the air.

# X is for boxcar.

Trains have pulled boxcars since the mid-1800s. Boxcars carry everything from vegetables to cattle.

**Y** is for
**yellow light**.

Red lights mean STOP.
Green lights mean GO.
Yellow lights tell drivers to
SLOW DOWN.

# Z is for zero to 60.

Sports cars are made for speed. Some can travel from zero to 60 miles (97 km) per hour in less than three seconds.

# Fun Facts about Transportation

 The colorful fabric bag on the top of a hot air balloon is called an envelope.

 The autobahn is a highway system in Germany. It has very few speed limits. Sports car drivers love to zoom along the autobahn.

 The first school buses weren't buses at all. They were wagons pulled by horses.

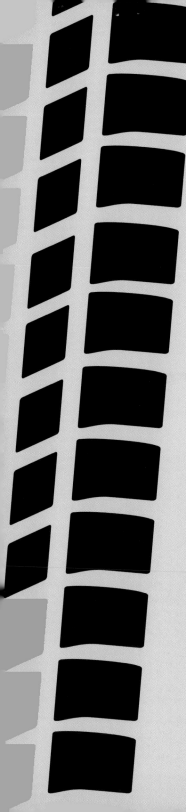

 President Barack Obama has his own special limo. The limo's body is super strong to keep the president safe. Its nickname is "The Beast."

 Some fire trucks raise ladders. Others have long hoses for spraying water. And some are made to take people to the hospital.

 Hybrid cars use both electricity and gas to run. Ferdinand Porsche made the world's first hybrid car in the early 1900s.

# Glossary

**electricity**—a form of energy used to power lights and other machines

**engineer**—a person who uses science and math to plan, design, or build

**gasoline**—a liquid fuel made from oil

**hybrid**—a mix of two different types; hybrid engines run on electricity and gasoline

**mechanic**—a person who fixes machines

**paramedic**—a person who treats sick and hurt people; paramedics travel in ambulances to places where people need treatment

**passenger**—someone besides the driver who travels in a car or other vehicle

**rescue**—to save someone who is in danger

**vehicle**—a machine that carries people and goods

# Read More

**Clark, Willow**. *Motorcycles on the Move*. Transportation Station. New York: PowerKids Press, 2010.

**Rustad, Martha E. H**. *Transportation in Many Cultures*. Life around the World. Mankato, Minn.: Capstone Press, 2009.

**Salas, Laura Purdie**. *Z Is for Zoom!: A Race Car Alphabet*. Alphabet Fun. Mankato, Minn.: Capstone Press, 2010.

# Internet Sites

FactHound offers a safe, fun way to find Internet sites related to this book. All of the sites on FactHound have been researched by our staff.

Here's all you do:

Visit *www.facthound.com*

FactHound will fetch the best sites for you!

# Index

9/10 E
Ipcizade

A+ Books are published by Capstone Press,
151 Good Counsel Drive, P.O. Box 669, Mankato, Minnesota 56002.
www.capstonepub.com

Books published by Capstone Press are manufactured with paper
containing at least 10 percent post-consumer waste.

*Library of Congress Cataloging-in-Publication Data*
Ipcizade, Catherine.
  H is for honk! : a transportation alphabet / by Catherine Ipcizade.
    p. cm.—(A+ books. Alphabet fun)
  Includes bibliographical references and index.
  Summary: "Introduces transportation themes through photographs and brief text that uses one word
relating to the subject for each letter of the alphabet"—Provided by publisher.
  ISBN 978-1-4296-4464-8 (library binding)
  1.  Motor vehicles—Juvenile literature. 2. Transportation—Juvenile literature. 3. Alphabet books. I. Title.
II. Series.
TL147.I63 2011
629.04—dc22                                                                      2010001357

## Credits

Megan Peterson, editor; Kyle Grenz, designer; Laura Manthe, production specialist

## Photo Credits

123RF/iofoto: 12, Lucian Coman, 18; Alamy/Michele Falzone: 15; Capstone Press/Gary Sundermeyer: 14,
Karon Dubke, 3, 7, 9; Getty Images Inc./The Image Bank/Cosmo Condina: 6 ; iStockphoto/bojan fatur: 16,
Kenneth C. Zirkel, 8, Mark Evans, 27, Nancy Louie, 23, photo75, 4, Slobo Mitic, 5; NASA: 19; Shutterstock/
Alex Neauville: 10, Bryant Jayme, 2, Dwight Smith, 17, Eduard Stelmakh, 28–29 (tire), emin kuliyev, 21,
Huguette Roe, 11, Kanwarjit Singh Boparai, cover, Konstantin Sutyagin, 13, Monkey Business Images,
1, Morgan Lane Photography, 20, Peter Weber, 25, Photography Perspectives - Jeff Smith, 22, Sasha
Radosavljevich, 24, Sue Smith, 26

## Note to Parents, Teachers, and Librarians

Alphabet Fun books use bold art and photographs and topics with high appeal to engage young children in
learning. Compelling nonfiction content educates and entertains while propelling readers toward mastery of
the alphabet. These books are designed to be read aloud to a pre-reader or read independently by an early
reader. The images help children understand the text and concepts discussed. Alphabet Fun books support
further learning by including the following sections: Fun Facts, Glossary, Read More, Internet Sites, and
Index. Early readers may need assistance using these features.